MERRILY ON HIGH

DVENT, CHRISTMAS & EPIPHANY ANTHEMS
FOR UPPER-VOICE CHOIRS

Selected & edited by Barry 1

NOVELLO
London

NOV 032121

Cover: "The Adoration of the Magi".
Detail from a stained-glass window in Holy Trinity Church, Sissinghurst, Kent,
designed and made in 1950 by Joseph E. Nuttgens (1892-1982).
Photograph: Peter Cormack.

Cover design: Michael Bell Design.

Music setting by Stave Origination.

ISBN 0-85360-956-X

Head office:
14-15 Berners Street,
London W1T 3LJ

Tel +44 (0)20 7612 7400
Fax +44 (0)20 7612 7545

Sales and Hire:
Music Sales Distribution Centre,
Newmarket Road,
Bury St Edmunds,
Suffolk IP33 3YB

Tel +44 (0)1284 702600
Fax +44 (0)1284 768301

www.musicsalesclassical.com
e-mail music@musicsales.co.uk

Contents

Preface

Welcome to this new collection of Advent, Christmas and Epiphany anthems, songs and carols for upper-voice choirs.

Music for these three seasons of the Christian year has always had a special place in services and concerts, in schools, colleges, concert-halls, churches and cathedrals. *Merrily on High* now adds to that wealth of texts and music from many centuries, as you sing of the symbolic progression from darkness to light through the season of Advent, the unrestrained joy of Christ's birth at Christmas and the coming of the Wise Men at Epiphany – culminating in the Presentation of Christ in the Temple (2nd February), for which we have included a setting of the Nunc Dimittis.

Although some of the items here have been published before, no fewer than eleven of them appear in print for the first time; some have been written for the book, whilst others are new arrangements of existing compositions.

With its previously published companion, *High Praise* (NOV 032118), here is a choice of beautiful words and music for choirs of all sizes and musical and vocal abilities. I hope you'll enjoy our selection and will find many new favourites for your own Advent, Christmas and Epiphany celebrations.

Barry Rose
Somerset, 1999

The following items are available on CD (Lammas LAMM 117).
Malcolm Archer: *Brightest and best*
Malcolm Archer: *Come, watch with us this Christmas night*
arr. A.E. Baker: *Whence is that goodly fragrance flowing?*
Mark Blatchly: *Magnificat in B flat*
arr. Andrew Parnell: *Rejoice and be merry*
Barry Rose: *An Advent responsory: I look from afar*
arr. Barry Rose: *Come, thou Redeemer of the earth*
Michael Rose: *Now the most high is born*

***Adam lay ybounden*: Michael Hurd** (b.1928)
This text is often sung in Advent, and also around the first Lesson (Genesis iii) in some Festivals of Nine Lessons and Carols. Michael Hurd's exciting musical setting was written for the 1965 Farnham Festival and first performed by the choir of Farnham Grammar School for Girls. It is one of a set of four pieces entitled *Canticle of the Blessed Virgin Mary*.

Adam lay ybounden will repay careful learning at a slow speed, especially for the tuning in bars 9-10, 14-15 etc. where the chording needs to be accurate. The first sopranos will need to work hardest in the opening phrases, since they sing the text before the other two parts. Check whether the words are clear enough – can the text 'four thousand winter thought he not too long?' be heard clearly? The accompaniment, conceived for piano, is also suitable for organ. (The composer has also orchestrated the piece for strings and woodwind.)
(Advent and Christmas carol services)

***An Advent Responsory*: Barry Rose** (b. 1934)
Advent Carol Services originated in the College chapels at Cambridge University, where term ends well before Christmas and students and staff of the Colleges wanted to worship together in chapel at a special seasonal service. Some of these services begin with an Advent responsory – an English translation of words attributed to the First Responsory at Matins on Advent Sunday from an ancient Roman rite, including part of Psalm 80. It is usually sung by the unaccompanied choir, in darkness or candlelight, to music adapted from Palestrina. I believe this is the first setting of these words specifically for upper voices. Try to achieve a gradual building in volume, from the opening solo to the full volume of the choir at the second repetition of 'Tell us, art thou he that should come to reign'. Although conventionally notated, the unison passages should have the flow of free speech-rhythm. It is usual to break after 'Tell us', though the only time it is really necessary to break after 'people' is in bar 20; hence the markings at that point.
(Advent Services, especially on the first Sunday)

***Come, thou Redeemer of the earth*: arr. Barry Rose**
In some Advent Carol Services this hymn immediately follows the Advent Responsory, sometimes sung by the choir and sometimes in procession. The words were written by St. Ambrose in the 4th century; the translation is by the 19th century cleric and scholar, John Mason Neale. The melody, adapted from Michael Praetorius, was originally sung to the German carol *Geboren ist Gottes Sönelein* and was matched to these words in the first edition of the *English Hymnal*. The organ/

piano introduction is optional, and the first verse may be sung by a group or a soloist. Take care not to let the singers 'grab' breath at the end of lines and make sure that the sense of the words in verse 2 (bar 19) is observed. The start of the last verse brings into focus the technique of singing two consonants which are the same – one ending a word and the other beginning the next – as in 'all laud'. The way to do this is to keep the tongue loose and then to build a small sound 'bridge' between the two consonants. Unheard by the listener, this is an '*er*' sound – say it slowly and you'll see what I mean. The final Amen should have the most singers on the third soprano (alto) part.
(*Suitable throughout Advent*)

Brightest and best: **Malcolm Archer** (b. 1952)
Reginald Heber wrote this Epiphany hymn in 1811 whilst he was Rector of Hodnet in Shropshire, and since then it has been included in many hymnals, with different tunes, as well being published in anthem form. I first heard Malcolm Archer's setting on a BBC Evensong some years ago, and since then it has become deservedly popular. The glittering organ part sets the mood for the choir and the music needs to keep moving – almost a feel of one in a bar. Choir directors and singers will need to be aware of the continuous pattern in the organ part, which means that some notes will be sung for less than their printed value (e.g. bars 12, 21, 29 etc.) if the musical flow is not to be interrupted. The first verse may be sung by a semi-chorus: the vocal lines should be legato, though the words need to be articulated clearly. For the vocalized 'Ah's you could use fewer voices, and in the final verse, I suggest that only the firsts sing the descant. If audibility of the final solo phrase is a problem, then the choir could always hum from bar 73 to the end.
Suitable for accompaniment on organ or piano.
(*Epiphany; or before/after carol service reading about the Wise Men*)

A child is born: **Peter Moorse** (b. 1930)
In 1959, whilst organist and choirmaster at St. Peter's Church, Morden, Surrey, Peter Moorse was asked to write a piece for an RSCM Deanery Festival. The text is translated from a Dutch carol – *Een kint gheboren in Bethlehem*. Originally scored for SATB choir and organ, the composer has made this new arrangement for upper-voice choirs. Approach the legato lines with great affection, and take care not to stress wrong syllables in such words as 'Bethlehem' (bar 4), and 'humanity' (bar 14). When learning the last verse, I suggest the second sopranos and altos learn their parts first, before the first sopranos sing over the top of them – there are a few dissonances here which need confidence in the lower parts. The solo at the end was specially written for Peter Moorse's head chorister at that time, who could comfortably sing up to the E above 'top' C! The composer suggests that if no soloist of yours is happy at this height, it could be played on a flute stop on the organ. The refrain means*: Love! how sweet is love!*
(*Christmas*)

Come, watch with us this Christmas night: **Malcolm Archer**
Bishop Timothy Dudley-Smith is one of the best known of contemporary hymn writers. Malcolm Archer has now written this new and melodious upper-voice setting of the first two verses. When I asked him for a word which would describe the musical and vocal approach needed, he replied 'relaxed' – and that's just what the voices will need to be, across the comparatively wide vocal range of a twelfth. The phrases should have an easy legato flow and we have made certain suggestions about breath or break points, which will help maintain that flow. The floating descant in verse 2 requires a very light touch, especially at that delicious musical 'crunch' in bar 61 – here the descant really needs to be just evident, and no more! The first verse presents quite a number of diction challenges to your choir, especially in a text which will be new to so many listeners; so persuade your singers to frame these words well, using tongue, teeth, lips and also taking care with words that begin with H.
(*Christmas*)

Down in yon forest: **arr. Tom Johnston**
We owe many of our well known carols to Ralph Vaughan Williams and the journeys he made in the early 1900s, collecting folk songs from around the country. This melody was from a Mr. Hall of Castleton in the Derbyshire Peak District and it flows like a tender lullaby. Tom Johnston's unaccompanied arrangement begins with a solo and ends with a fourth verse in four parts. This verse needs some careful tuning from an able semi-chorus and is in the form of a round. A good way to learn it is to get all three 'Lullay' parts to sing their first three phrases simultaneously; a good way of checking that all parts agree on the descending octave, the rising minor seventh, and so on. In the verse 2, soprano 2 and alto should sing in two-bar phrases, making each 'ding dong' distant and eerie. It may help achieve this if, when your singers reach the '*ng*' at the end of each word, they vocalise on that sound until it is time to sing the next '*di*' or '*do*'; that helps create a bell-like effect.
(*Christmas; also suitable for general use, using the bracketed word in verse 4*)

Fum, fum, fum: arr. **William Llewellyn**
Both William Llewellyn and I first heard this carol
on a broadcast choral Evensong from Liverpool
Cathedral, sometime in the early 1960s. Since then
its catchy tune has stayed with both of us and here it
is, in his arrangement for upper-voices. The original
words and melody are a traditional Catalan carol,
and it was first arranged for unaccompanied mixed
choir by Kurt Schindler (1882-1935). The
irrepressible march-like tempo is set in the short
introduction. 'Fum' may be a vocal representation of
a drum, and should be sung in a short, punchy way.
In your vocal enthusiasm, don't forget to observe the
piano in bar 36 which helps a gradual build-up to
the exciting ending. The pronounciation of the letter
u (in 'fum') will be more authentic and will sound
better as in 'umlaut' rather than 'fun'. The
accompaniment is suitable for piano or organ.
(*Advent and Christmas*)

Gabriel's message: arr. **William Llewellyn**
This beautiful Basque melody was probably
originally accompanied by just a vocal or
instrumental drone on one note. In the 1920s, with
some slight alterations to the notes of the melody, an
SATB harmonisation was added to the Rev. Sabine
Baring-Gould's translation of the original text. Our
new arrangement for upper voices is by William
Llewellyn, formerly Director of Music at
Charterhouse and editor of the 1986 *Novello Book
of Carols*. Note the different lengths of bars, which
point the singers towards the important syllables;
characterisation of the words will make a noticeable
difference to your interpretation. It is possible to use
a soloist in verse 1, and the lower part in verse 3
could be given to altos. In the last verse you will
need to make sure that the descant does not
overpower the tune. Accompaniment is equally
suited to piano or organ.
(*Christmas; also suitable for use around the Feast
of the Annunciation – 25th March*)

Go, tell it on the mountain: **John Abdenour**
(b. 1962)
Originally, the words of this piece may have been
secular, and even used as a way of secret
communication by slaves singing 'coded' messages
to each other. As soon as you hear the opening bars
of John Abdenour's rhythmic setting you'll probably
want to get up and dance – and why not? This is
ebullient writing, bringing to life the news of
Christ's birth, and your listeners should be able to
feel the joy in every chorus. By contrast, the
narrative verses are written in a more legato style, so
note the composer's instruction.
    John Abdenour lives in the USA and received
his early musical training as a chorister at St. Paul's

Cathedral, Detroit, later becoming associate organist
at Trinity Church, New Haven, Connecticut. He is
Director of Music at the First United Church of
Christ (Congregational) in Milford, Connecticut,
where he runs a flourishing adults' and children's
music programme. The accompaniment is suitable
for piano or organ.
(*Christmas*)

When Christ was born of Mary free: **John
Gardner** (b. 1917)
Here is an interesting and exciting combination of
15th century text with 20th century music, written
for two-part unaccompanied singing. John Gardner
was commissioned to write *When Christ was born of
Mary free* in 1962, for inclusion in *Sing Nowell*
(Novello). The composer describes the music as
'primitive' and I sometimes use the word
'forthright'. It needs to be sung in a rigid 4-beat
rhythm. Do not get faster from bar 12 onwards. To
keep the impetus going throughout the four verses, I
suggest that there is no slowing up at the end of each
chorus and that this one of those occasions when
singers and conductor should count between the
verses, in order to get the attack of the next one
absolutely together – perhaps a gap of 2 beats?
There are ways of pronouncing 'excelsis': for music
moving as fast as this, '<u>ek-shell</u>-cease' may be less
intrusive than '<u>ex-chel</u>-cease'.
(*Christmas and Epiphany*)

The holly and the ivy: arr. **Walford Davies/Wilson**
A well-known carol, collected by Cecil Sharp, who
wrote down the words and music of *The Holly and
the Ivy* from Mrs. Clayton, in Chipping Camden,
Gloucestershire. One of the most popular
arrangements was by Henry Walford Davies, for
SATB choir. In 1951 John Wilson (his nephew)
adapted the arrangement for upper voices, included
here. The music is cheerful and that should govern
the speed. At the start of line 2 ('of' in v. 1), both
soloists will need to rehearse carefully for ensemble.
In the chorus, persuade the choir to roll the 'R' of
'rising' – it will bring that word to life. Likewise,
persuade them to sing lightly and gracefully at 'the
playing of the merry organ', and this will nicely
point out the syncopation and triplet in the second
part. The ending needs carefully sustained legato
singing, and a beautiful sound to go with it – quite a
challenge! The accompaniment is equally suited to
piano or organ.
(*Christmas; also for general use, probably without
verse 4*)

How far is it to Bethlehem? **Geoffrey Shaw** (1879-
1943)
This quiet and thoughtful melody admirably matches

Frances Chesterton's 1920s poem. Geoffrey Shaw was a chorister at St. Paul's Cathedral and later studied with Charles Wood and Stanford at Cambridge. When he wrote this piece he was organist of St. Mary's Church, Primrose Hill, London, and his interest in collecting and editing folk songs probably influenced his writing. Originally for single voice, this three-part version dates from 1924. The feeling is similar to a lullaby. I suggest that a soloist might be used at bars 5, 7, 9 and 11, in which case, the opening four bars ought to be hummed, rather than sung to 'Ah'. To many choirs, the letter 'p' is elusive – at the end of such words as 'sheep' (bar 14), 'asleep' (bar 16), 'weep' (bar 28) . If those 'p's are to be audible to your listeners, they must be voiced – said, using the lips. (*Christmas*)

Magnificat in B flat: Mark Blatchly (b. 1960)
The words of the Magnificat and Nunc Dimittis are full of contrasts. Mark Blatchly's atmospheric setting was written in 1978 and dedicated to the choristers of St. Paul's Cathedral, where he had just completed a year as organ scholar. The delicate mood at the opening is highlighted by the unaccompanied three-part writing at 'and holy is his name'. The section at 'and his mercy' (and also at 'he remembering his mercy') is also peaceful and may be sung by a soloist or a semi-chorus, whilst all the choir need to give full force to the powerful 'he hath shewèd strength with his arm'. This piece (and the companion Nunc Dimittis) will well reward the careful preparation needed by both choir and organist. The accompaniment is best suited to the organ, but may be played as a piano duet.
(*Canticle from the Office of Evensong; also sung in some Advent and Christmas Carol Services following the lesson telling of The Annunciation. Suitable also for Feasts of the Blessed Virgin Mary*)

Nunc Dimittis in B flat: Mark Blatchly
You might like to teach this to your choir before tackling the Magnificat, because it is shorter and will introduce them to the composer's idiom and cover some musical ground common to both Canticles. The Gloria is common to both, and the opening phrase here is also used at 'he remembering his mercy' in the Magnificat. Again, getting the right mood and speed is all important: peaceful at the opening (preferably with a soloist, but could also be sung by a small group). Take care to observe the composer's dynamic markings at bars 10-16 – those singing the second part should be more audible than the firsts. The parts become equal at 'for mine eyes' and care needs to be taken to observe the sudden *mp* at 'which thou hast prepared'. The accompaniment encourages the singers to be jubilant at 'to be a

light' whilst they should also continue the legato of the accompaniment at 'and to be the glory'. A particularly beautiful effect is created by the return of the opening 'Lord, now lettest thou thy servant' and the quiet murmuring of the choir at 'in peace'. (*Canticle from the Office of Evensong; also sung as an anthem around the Feast of the Presentation of Christ in the Temple (2nd February) and at some funeral/memorial services*).

Myn lyking: R.R. Terry (1865-1938)
Between 1909 and 1911 Terry completed a collection of *Twelve Christmas Carols*, which he dedicated to his wife. At that time he was Director of Music at Westminster Cathedral and in the preface, he wrote 'a tune can only become a carol the nearer it approximates to the folk-song type and the further it departs from the hymn-tune'. Perhaps this is the best clue as to how to perform *Myn Lyking*, since it needs a simple folk song-like approach. The words are taken from the late 14th/early 15th century Sloane Manuscript in the British Library. The music was originally set for verses sung by upper voices, with an SATB chorus. In this new arrangement, the sopranos sing the verses, whilst the chorus is for SSAA which should, if possible, be unaccompanied. The pronounciation of the letter 'u' in 'Lullay' is a matter of taste. Some prefer it as in the word full, whilst others prefer it as in the word dull. (I have always used the latter).
(*Christmas: also suitable for some Feast-Days of the Blessed Virgin Mary*)

No room at the inn: D.A. Connett (b. 1927), arr. Barry Rose
Amongst my music, I have two scraps of paper on which Tony Connett (headmaster of Bramdean School, Exeter) sent me his words and the sketch for the melody of *No room at the inn*. Soon after I had arranged it for the school's chapel choir, it was recorded in aid of the Bosnian Children's Appeal, and sold over 60,000 copies. This new arrangement for upper voices retains the same musical pattern as the original. The accompaniment is suitable for piano, organ or harp-like sounds. It's a delightful and memorable tune with a real 'tinsel' feel. The vocalised parts are an integral part of the original arrangement and I think you will find that they add something extra to this version.
(*Suitable for Christmas/Epiphany*)

Now the most high is born: Michael Rose (b. 1934)
I first heard Michael Rose's (no relation) memorable and rhythmic setting of *Now the most high is born* sung by the choir of Belmont School, Mill Hill, London in 1976. The piece is dedicated to the choir of Clifton High School for Girls, conductor Sheila

Forster and accompanist John Marsh. Written with piano accompaniment, it may also be played on organ. The 15th century poem by James Ryman is macaronic (a mixture of English and Latin): it tells of the announcement of Christ's birth to the shepherds and their journey to Bethlehem to see the new-born babe. You'll soon sense that the music perfectly matches every mood of the text as it moves from its home key G minor through various other keys. These key changes are something of which your choir will need to be aware. The piece requires vocal stamina and technique, an acute awareness of the contrasting moods of the text and an understanding of how to put these across to your listeners. Diction is all important. The ending is vibrant and vital and should *not* slow down. Be careful not to oversing at this point, for the sake of the tuning.
(*Christmas; also suitable for concerts/recitals in church or hall*)

O this night is born Noël: **Gerald Cockshott** (1915-79)

A 17th century French carol, translated and harmonised in the 1950s. Cockshott had studied composition with Vaughan Williams, and taught English at Whittinghame College, Sussex. Suitable as a solo song, this attractive melody may flow better in French, though your singers may need some careful coaching in their pronunciation – especially at the refrain. The tessitura of the outer verses is suitable for both soprano and alto, but the range of the second verse is only suited to the higher sopranos. It may take some time to get used to the key-changes at bars 22-23 and 41-42. Accompanists can help these transitions with a hint of rubato at these points.
(*Christmas*)

People look east: **arr. Barry Rose**

This charming French melody first appeared in a 19th century collection of carols published by Novello, compiled by the Rev. H.R. Bramley and John Stainer. There it was matched to a Christmas text based on an old French carol *Shepherds, shake off your drowsy sleep*, but in the *Oxford Book of Carols* (1928) a new set of words by Eleanor Farjeon was used. In this new arrangement, the mood is set by a firm and jaunty rhythm of the accompaniment – a lead which the choir will certainly follow. Verse 2 presents the sopranos with all sorts of challenges to their diction and it might be a good idea in rehearsal to get them to *say* the text, in rhythm, and see how many of the words can be understood. Note that the first soprano is the only one of the three parts to sing the word 'rose' (bar 27) – and I'm always very keen on this word being

clearly sung! This second verse could be accompanied by a light continuo part. Verse 4 also has a punctuation problem: there should be a small break in bar 35 after 'word', and then a firmer attack on 'The Lord is coming'; this always takes some some rehearsing. In the final three bars make sure that the descant is not louder than the melody; here those on the tune are the only ones to sing the key-word 'Lord'.
(*Suitable throughout Advent*)

Two Polish carols: **Witold Lutoslawski** (1913-94)

Lutoslawski wrote this set of 20 Polish Christmas carols in 1946. Based on traditional Polish melodies they are scored for unison voices with a piano accompaniment which often seems to be independent in tonality from the vocal lines. *Hurrying to Bethlehem* is a simple melody, but your singers will need to be sure of its tonality before the accompaniment is added, and it is then that they will enjoy Lutoslawki's 'opposing' but complementary piano writing. The singers should keep the words light and on the tip of their tongue and teeth, and for the sake of clarity of diction, it might help to get the choir to say the text in rhythm before they sing it.

Many will immediately recognise the melody of *In a Manger* from its later adaptation to *Infant Holy, infant lowly.* Here is a much gentler and more flowing accompaniment. Again the melody is easy to learn and should be sung delicately and with great affection for the right word stresses. The original Polish has been included, for adventurous choirs.
(*Christmas*)

Rejoice and be merry: **arr. Andrew Parnell**

This text and dance-like melody are taken from an old tune book found in a Dorset church. The cheerful tune is very similar to the Cornish melody for *Tomorrow shall be my dancing day*, (see p. 120) and the words suggest that it was a traditional carol for Christmas morning. We have taken the liberty of providing some alternatives in the first verse which also make it suitable for Epiphany. It was the Reverend J.T. Darwall who gave *Rejoice and be merry* to the editors of the 1919 *English Carol Book*, since when it has reappeared many times. This new arrangement for two-part choir is by Andrew Parnell, founder and Musical Director of the St. Albans Abbey Girls' Choir, to whom it is dedicated. The music should move with a happy lilt, with that one-in-a-bar feeling, though your choir will need to be careful not to put more than one vocal stress in each of those bars – otherwise it will gradually slow down and also give the effect of 'chattering' – i.e. 'birth-DAY OF Je-SUS OUR King'. The words need to be quickly and properly framed: use the tongue, teeth and lips a little more than usual, and

take extra care that the ends of the phrases are not shortened so much that they sound grabbed. In the last verse, make sure that the descant does not overpower the melody. The accompaniment may be played on either piano or organ, and the introductory phrase may be omitted.
(*Christmas Day, or at other times, using the alternative text provided in verse 1*)

The shepherds' farewell: **Hector Berlioz** (1803-69) **arr. Basil Ramsey**

Berlioz's choral trilogy, *L'enfance du Christ* was written over a period of four years, and from it comes this well known chorus, *L'Adieu des bergers*. Originally scored for SATB chorus and orchestra, this was the first movement to be composed. At the first performance in 1850, Berlioz passed it off as the work of an unknown 17th century composer. Paul England's translation is well known in the SATB version, and now it is included here in Basil Ramsey's arrangement for three-part upper voices. The Allegretto marking is the composer's and is a reminder not to take the piece too slowly. The opening bars are reminiscent of shepherds' pipes and the essence of the text is one of movement – depicting the somewhat hasty departure from the stable by the Holy Family. Take care with the intervals and tuning in the second soprano and alto parts in bars 27-30 and corresponding spots in the other verses.
(*Christmas*)

Say, where is He born? **Felix Mendelssohn** (1809-47)

There may be a few raised eyebrows at the inclusion of this piece in a book for upper-voices: the original is a minor 6th lower and scored for male voices, but we hope that upper-voice choirs will enjoy the opportunity to sing this transposed version, with its Epiphany-tide text. It comes from the late unfinished oratorio *Christus* and tells of the Wise Men as they follow the star that guides them to the infant Jesus. Remember to aim for a natural speech-like flow in the recitative. The trio is suitable for soloists or the whole choir; be aware of the slight articulation needed between 'say' and 'where' each time those two words appear. It's difficult to get word clarity at the phrase 'for we have seen his star' - mainly because of the 'v' in 'have' and achieving the link from 'his' to 'star', with the 'z' of 'his' and the 's' of 'star'.
(*Epiphany; or around a carol service lesson about the Wise Men*)

Silent night: **Franz Gruber** (1787-1853) **arr. Mark Blatchly**

Silent Night, one of world's best loved carols, was first performed on Christmas Eve, 1818 in the Austrian town of Oberndorf by its writers, Joseph Mohr and Franz Gruber. Whatever the legends that have grown up as to why it was written, we know that the original had six verses and was accompanied on a guitar, using just three common chords. Mark Blatchly made this arrangement for a 1980 recording by Paul Phoenix and his fellow choristers at St. Paul's Cathedral, accompanied by organ and orchestra. The version published here is a reduction of the orchestral score, retaining the original voice parts. I suggest that Voices II in the first verse might be a mixture of second sopranos and first altos, whilst the lower part in the second verse should definitely be sung by the altos. The choir parts in the first verse may be quietly doubled by the accompaniment, if support is needed. The accompaniment can be played as a piano duet.
(*Christmas*)

Still, still, still: **arr. Barry Rose**

A delicate and charming cradle song from Germany. Here is a translation of the text:
1. Be quiet, the baby wants to sleep. Mary sings until the baby sleeps. She will comfort him with breast-milk.
2. Sleep my lovely baby, sleep! The angels are already making music to celebrate the baby's birth.
3. We are surrounded by the greatest love of all.
God has left his throne in Heaven to be amongst us. The music is gentle and flowing and that mood is set in the introduction – organists should not use pedals until bar 10. Although given a time-signature of 4/4, most bars require the singers to think in minims/half-notes in order to avoid wrong word stresses. The divisi marked in verse 2 can be varied according to the forces available (alto 1 might include some sopranos). As in all descants, please be sure that the 'Ah's do not dominate and are quietly floated over the top of the melody. The half speed ending from bar 50 onwards may need some careful rehearsal.
(*Christmas and Epiphany*)

Sweet was the song: **Gerald Hendrie** (b. 1935)

Sometimes known *as The Lute Book Lullaby*, the words have been attributed to William Ballet. Gerald Hendrie's delicate music is a perfect match to the poem and depicts the gentle rocking of the cradle both in the accompaniment and the vocal writing. It was first published in 1966. The art of singing this well relies on both the conductor and the singers thinking of one beat in each bar, rather than three – that way you will get the right vocal and musical flow. Where the text has no commas (i.e. bars 10 and 39) choir directors may decide to 'carry over', though I would suggest the smallest of articulations would be possible at these points. Intonation can be uneasy in the key of F major – so please take care to tune the falling semitones, and especially in the 'Lulla' phrases. (for pronounciation alternatives for this word, see *Myn Lyking*: Richard Terry) (*Christmas: also suitable following some Old Testament readings in Advent Carol services*)

Tomorrow shall be my dancing day: arr. Andrew Carter

Historically, carols are linked with dancing, and nowhere is that more apparent than in this jolly dance-like tune – set to words that are all about dancing! *Tomorrow shall be my dancing day* originates from Cornwall and charts the story of Christ's life, from his birth, through his death to his ascension. In this version, only the Christmas verses have been set. Andrew Carter made this effective and enjoyable arrangement in the early 1970s. Note his instruction about lightness (both in the accompaniment and singing); choir directors may need to take extra care with the descant in the second verse where the duplets may easily become too heavy and turn back into triplets. The final verse presents extra challenges with diction and here the words have to be even clearer than usual, in view of the imitative writing for the second sopranos in that verse. After the accompaniment suddenly stops in bar 51, the choir should sing its final three bars with great confidence and panache, whilst also paying careful attention to the tuning of those sustained chords. Originally intended for piano accompaniment, this is also suitable for the organ. (*Christmas and general use*)

Torches! John Joubert (b. 1927)

Here is one of the best known of all modern carol settings. In the early 1950s, John Joubert taught at the University of Hull, and wrote *Torches* for the annual carol service at a local girls' school. Set for piano and unison voices with an optional second part, it was published in the well-known SATB version and became known to millions through its inclusion in the festival of Nine Lessons and Carols in the chapel of King's College, Cambridge. Now the composer has made this new arrangement for *Merrily on High*. The original text is Spanish; this English translation was made in the 1920s by J.B. Trend for the *Oxford Book of Carols*. From the opening chords of the accompaniment there is an immediate sense of urgency and the more gentle mood of verse 2 is beautifully portrayed by the sustained chords in the accompaniment. The third verse creates excitement through the use of two-part writing. You will need very energised singing, taking care not to grab at the end of phrases. Two small reminders about the first verse: i) be careful not to put the stress on the second syllable of 'Torches' –

or your listeners will hear 'Tor-CHES'. ii) 'Bethlehem' is just one word – here I've often heard choirs punch out each syllable, which does *not* sound good! (*Christmas*)

Watts's Cradle Hymn: Barry Rose

Known as the 'father of English Hymnody', Isaac Watts (1674-1748) wrote around 600 hymns including this delightful cradle song. Four of the original seven verses are now featured in this new setting which, with its 6/8 time signature, seeks to depict the gentle rocking of the cradle. One practical tip is to work with your choir on the letter H – there are four 'H' leads on the first page. This does not need to be overdone; the choir needs to breathe out as it begins to sing the letter, otherwise your listeners may only hear *'ush* (bar 3), *'oly* (bar 5) *'eavenly* (bar 7) etc. In the last verse you will need to have more singers on the second part so that the descant does not dominate the melody. Some of those singing the tune could go to the second part in bar 36 to help balance the last chord. Written for piano accompaniment, this also suits the organ. (*Christmas and general use*)

Whence is that goodly fragrance flowing? arr. A.E. Baker

This 17th century French carol first became known in the early 18th century when the tune was included in John Gay's *Beggar's Opera*. This arrangement dates from 1930 and is dedicated to the Choristers of the Lower Chapel at Eton College. The English text is by A.B.Ramsay. I'm tempted to wonder if this is the Allan Ramsay (1686-1758) whose Scottish pastoral comedy *The Gentle Shepherd* is said to have inspired the writing of the *Beggar's Opera*. Baker's timeless arrangement paints the pastoral nature of the words and music, whilst adding a sense of urgency with the imitative entries at 'run ye with eager footsteps hieing'. It's one of those pieces which needs great warmth and affection in the singing, and although verse 2 is marked as a solo, it may be sung by a semi-chorus or full choir. You will need to take care with the punctuation in bars 35 and 36 – the arranger has clearly marked the sense of the words. The accompaniment is best suited to the organ. (*Christmas*)

Adam lay ybounden

15th century

Michael Hurd

And all was for an ap-ple, an ap-ple that he took,

And all was for an ap-ple, an ap-ple that he

And all was for an ap-ple, an ap-ple that he

As clerk-ës find-en writ-ten in their book.

took, As clerk - ës find-en writ-ten in their book.

took, As clerk - ës find-en writ-ten in their book.

Ne had the ap-ple tak-en been, the ap-ple tak-en been,

Ne had the ap-ple tak-en been, the ap-ple tak-en been,

Ne had the ap-ple tak-en been, the ap-ple tak-en been,

For Malcolm Archer and the girl choristers of Wells Cathedral

An Advent responsory: I look from afar

Words translated from an early rite
of the Office of Matins for Advent Sunday

Barry Rose

18 ALL SOPRANOS ✓ Is - ra - el.

Stir up thy strength, O Lord, and come to reign over thy peo - ple, Is - ra - el.

23 ALL SOLOISTS

Glory be to the Fa - ther, and to the Son, and to the Ho - ly Ghost.

25

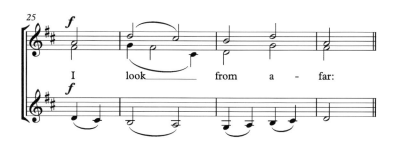

I look from a - far:

29 ALL SOPRANOS

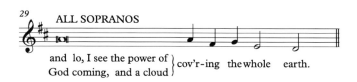

and lo, I see the power of God coming, and a cloud } cov'r-ing the whole earth.

30 ALL *ff*

Go ye out to meet him, and say: Tell us, art thou he that should come to reign over thy

32 Is - - ra - el.

Peo - ple Is - ra - el.

In many Advent Carol Services, the hymn *Come, thou Redeemer of the earth* now follows.

For Patrick Aiken and the children's choir of the First United Church of Christ, Providence, USA

Come, thou Redeemer of the earth

St. Ambrose,
translated J.M. Neale & others

Melody adapted by Michael Praetorius
arr. Barry Rose

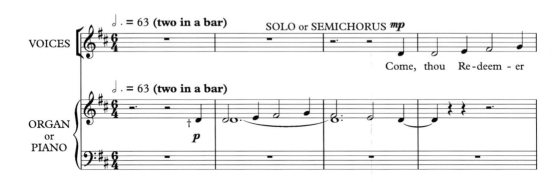

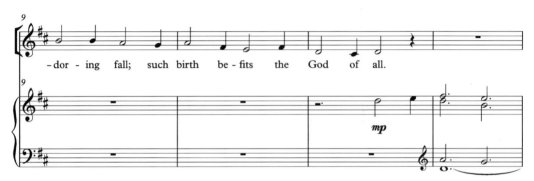

† Optional introduction: see Editor's notes.

A FEW MORE VOICES

Be - got - ten of no

hu - man will, But of the Spi - rit, thou art still the Word of God in

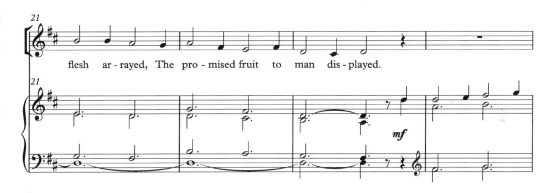

flesh ar - rayed, The pro - mised fruit to man dis - played.

FULL *mf*

O e - qual to thy Fa - ther, thou! Gird

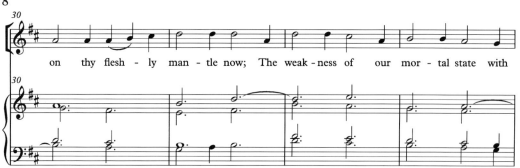

on thy flesh - ly man - tle now; The weak - ness of our mor - tal state with

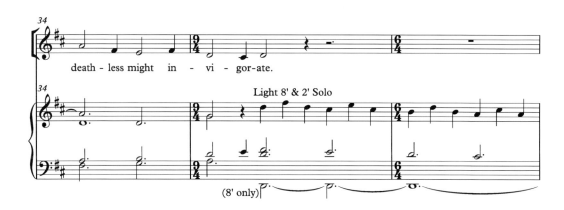

death - less might in - vi - gor-ate.

Light 8' & 2' Solo

(8' only)

FULL *mp*

Thy cra - dle here shall glit - ter bright, And

dark - ness breathe a new - er light, Where end - less faith shall shine se - rene, And

* If played on piano, repeat low D at these points.

* If played on piano, repeat low D at these points.

For Phillip Bell and the boys of Eccles Hall School, Norfolk, England

Brightest and best

Reginald Heber

Malcolm Archer

Con moto (♩ = 120)

(Gt. or Ch.) bright registration

ORGAN

mp

Ped.

1st time SOLO, 2nd time ALL

mf

mf

Bright - est and best of the sons of the morn - ing,
Cold on his cra - dle the dew - drops are shin - ing;

dawn on our dark - ness and lend us thine aid;
low lies his head with the beasts of the stall;

star of the east, the ho - ri - zon a - dorn - ing,
an - gels a - dore him in slum - ber re - clin - ing,

guide where our in - fant Re - deem - er is laid.
Ma - ker and Mon - arch and Sa - viour of

all. Say, shall we yield him in cost - ly de -

-vo - tion, o - dours of E - dom, and offer - ings di -

-vine, gems of the moun - tain, and pearls of the

o - cean, myrrh from the for - est, or gold from the

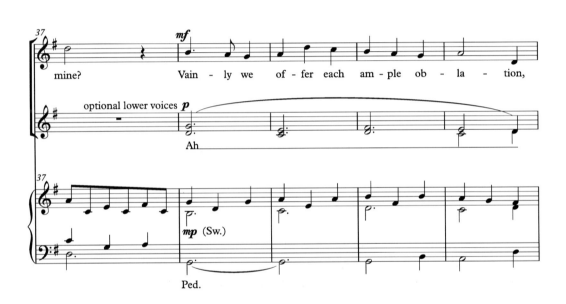

mine?   Vain - ly we of - fer each am - ple ob - la - tion,

mf

optional lower voices *p*

Ah

mp (Sw.)

Ped.

vain - ly with gifts would his fa - vour se - cure: rich - er by

Ah   Ah

A child is born

R.C. Trevelyan

Peter Moorse

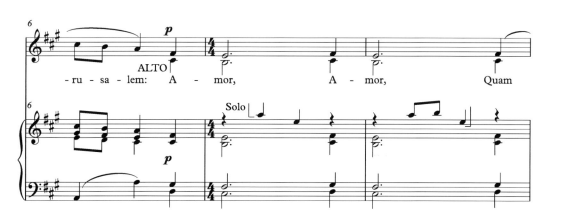

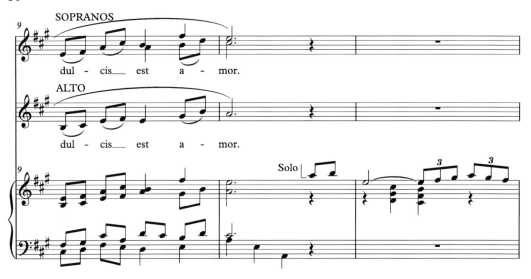

dul - cis___ est a - mor.

dul - cis___ est a - mor.

Solo

The Son took up - on___ Him hu - ma - ni - ty that to the

Manuals

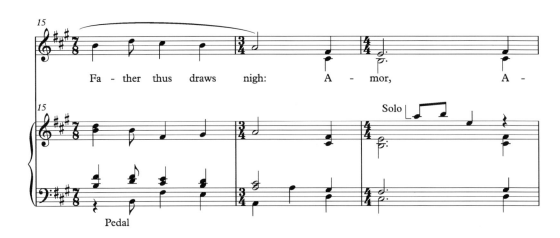

Fa - ther thus draws nigh: A - mor, A -

Solo

Pedal

For Nigel McClintock and the boys of St. George's Parish Church, Belfast

Come, watch with us this Christmas night

Timothy Dudley-Smith

Malcolm Archer

FULL SOPRANO I *p*

Ah_____ Ah_____

FULL SOPRANO II *mp*

Who would not join the an - gel songs that tell the

Sa - viour's birth?_____ The Lord_ for whom cre - a - tion

Ah_____ Ah_____

longs, has come at last_ to earth;_____ the full - ness

Ah_____

Down in yon forest

collected R. Vaughan Williams
arr. Tom Johnston

Fum, fum, fum

trad. Catalan
arr. William Llewellyn

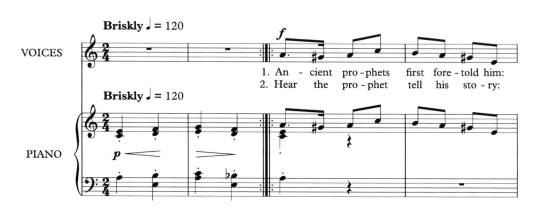

Gabriel's message

S. Baring-Gould

trad. Basque
arr. William Llewellyn

hail,' said he, 'thou low - ly maid - en Ma - ry,___ Most
Son shall be Em - ma - nu - el, by seers fore - told.___

high - ly fa - vour'd la - dy,' Glo - - - ri - a!

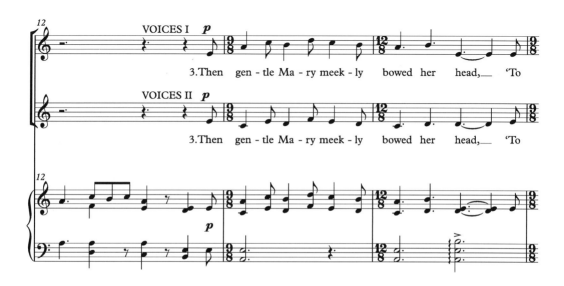

VOICES I

3.Then gen - tle Ma - ry meek - ly bowed her head,___ 'To

VOICES II

3.Then gen - tle Ma - ry meek - ly bowed her head,___ 'To

Go, tell it on the mountain

Negro spiritual

John Abdenour

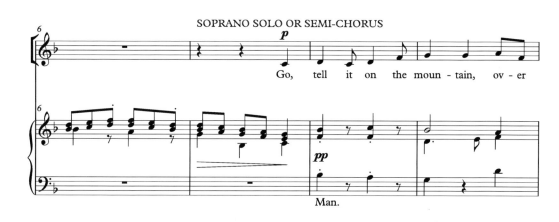

36

hold through out the hea-vens there shone a ho-ly light.

Go, tell it on the moun-tain, ov-er

Man.

hill and e-very-where; Go, tell it on the moun-tain that

Je-sus Christ is born.

* The lower octave notes should be used only if the upper octave is impractical

God sent us sal - va - tion ___ that ___ bles - sed Christ - mas morn.
(this)

Sw. to mixt.

p

cresc. Gt. Add

FULL *f*

Go, tell it on the moun - tain, ov - er

hill and e - very-where; Go, tell it on the moun - tain that

ff

When Christ was born of Mary free

15th century

John Gardner

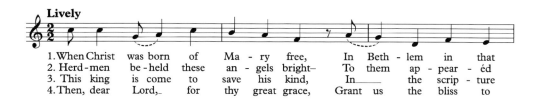

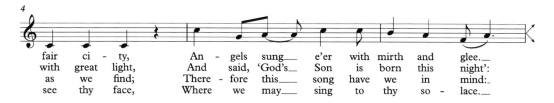

Lively

1. When Christ was born of Ma - ry free, In Beth - lem in that
2. Herd - men be - held these an - gels bright— To them ap - pear - éd
3. This king is come to save his kind, In the scrip - ture
4. Then, dear Lord, for thy great grace, Grant us the bliss to

fair ci - ty, An - gels sung e'er with mirth and glee.
with great light, And said, 'God's Son is born this night':
as we find; There - fore this song have we in mind:
see thy face, Where we may sing to thy so - lace.

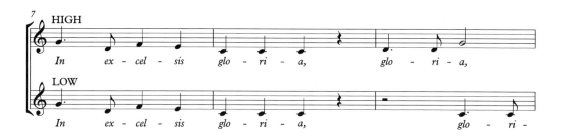

HIGH

In ex - cel - sis glo - ri - a, glo - ri - a,

LOW

In ex - cel - sis glo - ri - a, glo - ri -

glo - ri - a, in ex - cel - sis glo - ri - a, Chris -

-a, glo - ri - a, in ex - cel - sis glo - ri - a,

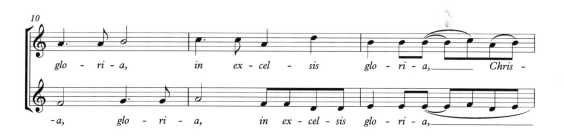

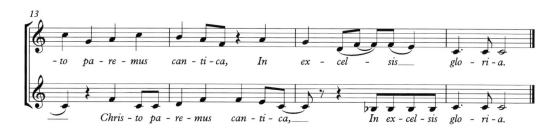

- to pa - re - mus can - ti - ca, In ex - cel - sis glo - ri - a.

Chris - to pa - re - mus can - ti - ca, In ex - cel - sis glo - ri - a.

The holly and the ivy

trad., arr. Walford Davies
adapted John Wilson

SOPRANO I

1. The Hol - ly and the I - vy When they are both full grown;
2. The Hol - ly bears a blos - som As white as an - y flower;
*3. The Hol - ly bears a ber - ry As red as an - y blood;
4. The Hol - ly bears a pric - kle As sharp as an - y thorn;
*5. The Hol - ly bears a bark As bitter as an - y gall;

SOPRANO II or ALTO

Of all the trees that are in the wood The Hol - ly bears the
And Ma - ry bore sweet Je - sus Christ To be our sweet Sa -
And Ma - ry bore sweet Je - sus Christ To do poor sin - ners
And Ma - ry bore sweet Je - sus Christ On Christ - mas day in the
And Ma - ry bore sweet Je - sus Christ For to re - deem us

crown.
-viour.
good.
morn.
all.

O the ris - ing of the sun and the run - ning of the

CHORUS

O the ris - ing of the sun and the run - ning of the

* Alternative ALTO SOLO for Verses 3 & 5

DUET

3. The Hol - ly bears a ber - ry As red as an - y blood; And Ma - ry bore....
5. The Hol - ly bears a bark As bitter as an - y gall; And Ma - ry bore....

43

How far is it to Bethlehem?

Frances Chesterton

Geoffrey Shaw

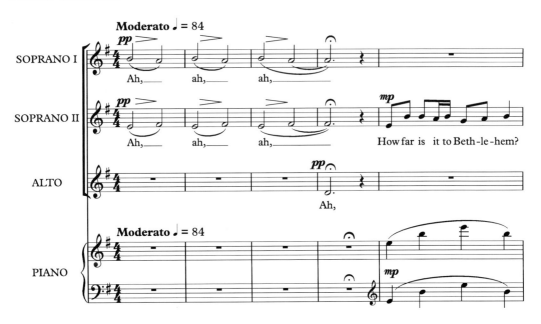

For Barry Rose and the Choristers of St. Paul's Cathedral

Magnificat and Nunc Dimittis

Magnificat

Mark Blatchly

Sa - viour. For he hath re - gard - ed the

low - li - ness of his hand - maid - en.

For be - hold, from hence - forth all ge - ne -

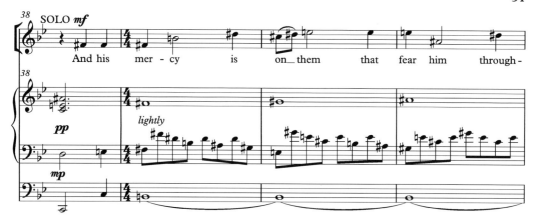

And his mer - cy is on them that fear him through-

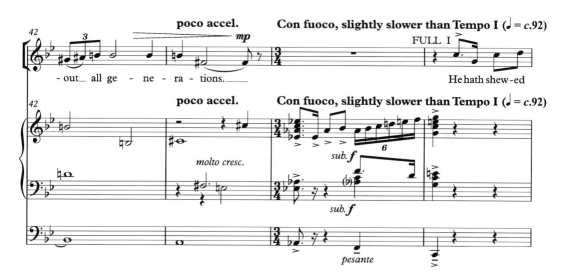

poco accel.

Con fuoco, slightly slower than Tempo I (♩ = c.92)

-out all ge - ne - ra - tions. He hath shew-ed

strength with his arm, with his arm:

FULL II

He hath shew-ed strength with his arm:

Tpt.

Thick and heavy

hun - gry with good things: and the rich___ he hath sent
emp-ty a - way. He___ re-
-mem-b'ring his mer - cy hath hol-pen his ser - vant Is - ra -

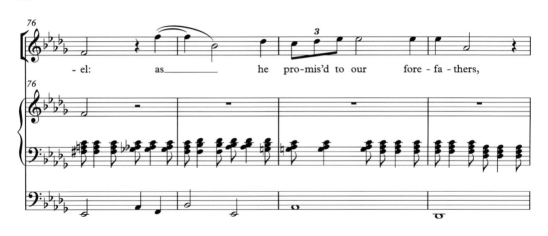

- el: as_____ he pro-mis'd to our fore-fa-thers,

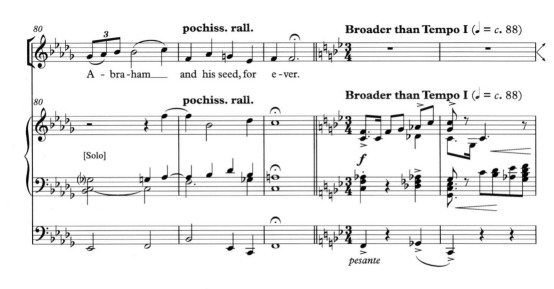

pochiss. rall. **Broader than Tempo I** (♩ = c. 88)

A - bra-ham_____ and his seed, for e -ver.

[Solo]

f

pesante

I f

Glo - ry be to the Fa - ther,_____ and to the_ Son:_

II ff

Glo - ry be_____ to the Fa -ther, and_

pesante

and to the Ho - ly Ghost;

to the Son: and to the Ho - ly Ghost;

As it was in the be - gin - ning, is

As it was in the be - gin - ning, is now and e - ver shall be:

SOLO

A - men.

now and e - ver shall be: world with - out end. A - men.

world with - out end. A - men.

+ 32'

Nunc Dimittis

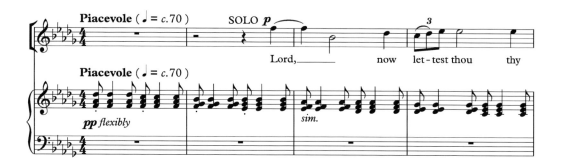

58

Myn lyking

15th century

R.R. Terry

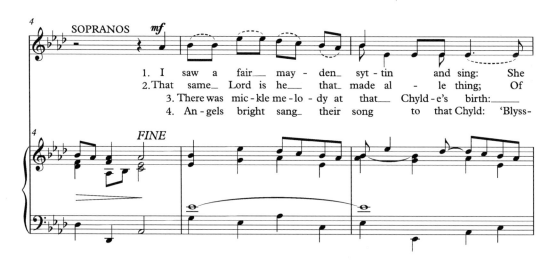

1. I saw a fair_ may - den_ syt - tin_ and sing: She
2. That same_ Lord is he_ that_ made al - le thing; Of
3. There was mic - kle me - lo - dy at that_ Chyld - e's birth:_
4. An - gels bright sang_ their song to that Chyld: 'Blyss-

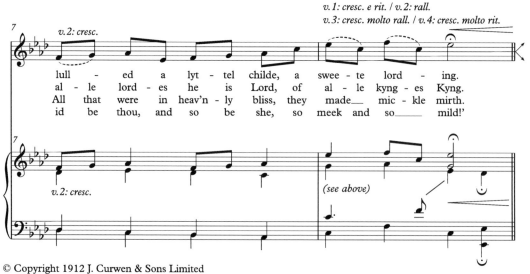

lull — ed a lyt - tel childe, a swee - te lord - ing.
al - le lord - es he is Lord, of al - le kyng - es Kyng.
All that were in heav'n - ly bliss, they made_ mic - kle mirth.
id be thou, and so be she, so meek and so__ mild!'

v.1: cresc. e rit. / v.2: rall.
v.3: cresc. molto rall. / v.4: cresc. molto rit.

* Refrain preferably unaccompanied

For Donald Hanson and the Chapel Choir of Bramdean School

No room at the inn
(The Exeter Carol)

D.A. Connett

Melody by D.A. Connett, arr. Barry Rose

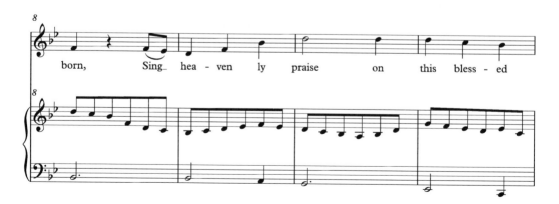

morn, Wise men from the east jour-neyed from_____ a -

- far,_____ They__ fol - lowed the light of the star._____

ALL SOPRANOS

_____ O bless - ed Ma - ry, vir - gin, maid - en

mild, Sweet mo - ther of_____ man - kind;

Boy Je-sus is born to save us from sin, In a

In a

sta - ble, no room at the inn. O_ sleep, gen - tle

sta - ble, no room at the inn.

child, a - sleep_ in the hay, God's crea-tures a - round,_ they will not

(S II/A semi-chorus) (p)

Oo (or Hum)

* one or two voices on each part

For Sheila Forster, Clifton High and John Marsh

Now the most high is born

Nunc natus est altissimus

James Ryman

Michael Rose

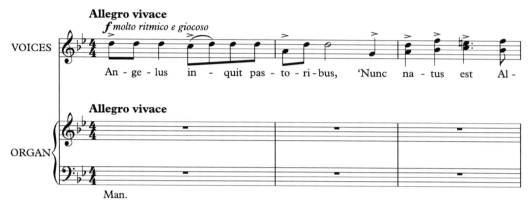

Man.

The angel said to the shepherds 'Now the most high is born'.

Upon a night an angel bright

Pas-to-ri-bus ap-pa-ru-it,___ And a-non right, thro'

to the shepherds he appeared

God-des might, Lux mag-na il-lis cla-ru-it:___

a great light shone around them

For love of us (Scrip-ture say-eth thus) Nunc na-tus est Al-

now the most high is born.

- tis - si - mus.

And of that light that was so bright Hic val-de ti - mu -

- e - runt; A sign of bliss to us it is,___

this filled them with fear

Hæc lux quam hic vi – de – runt: For love of us

the light you see here Man.

(Scrip - ture say - eth thus) Nunc na - tus est Al - tis - si - mus.

now the most high is born. Ped.

'Dread ye no - thing, great

joy I bring, Quod er - it om – ni po - pu - lo, For

which will be to all peoples

good Jo - seph and Ma - ry mild_ Po - si - tum_ in præ-

laid down in the

- se - pi - o_____ You shall find that hea - ven - ly child_

manger Ped.

Qui cæ - li præ - est so - li - o.'___ For love of us

sitting on the throne of heaven

(Scrip-ture say - eth thus) Nunc na - tus est Al - tis - si - mus._

now the most high is born.

The an-gel sung then with ma — ny more, 'Glo-ri — a, in al-

glory in the highest

-tis — si — mis!__ In earth be peace to man al-so__

Et gau-di-um sit an-ge-lis.'__ For love of us

and let there be joy to the angels

(Scrip-ture say-eth thus) Nunc na-tus est Al-tis — si — mus.__

now the most high is born.

na - tus est Al - tis - si - mus.

the most high is born.

TUTTI

poco f

When in such wise found

Man.

him they had__ Ut dic-tum est per an - ge-lum,__

as it was said by the angel

A - gain they came, and were full glad,__ Ma - gni - fi - can - tes

praising

78

O this night is born Noël

Cette nuit est né Noël

French 17th century

trad. French melody
arr. & English words by Gerald Cockshott

night is born No - ël, As the pro - phets did fore -
nuit est né No - ël Dans u - ne jo - lie mai -

- tell, In a sta - ble by the way___ Poor - ly
- son, Dans une cham - bre de pa - ra - de, Qui é -

Taken from *Noël! Chantons Noël!* by Paul Arma, Editions Ouvrières, Paris.
© Copyright 1955 Novello & Company Limited

82

People, look east

Eleanor Farjeon

Besançon melody
arr. Barry Rose

SOPRANO I

2. Fur-rows, be glad, though earth is bare, One more seed is plant - ed there:

SOPRANO II

2. Fur-rows, be glad, though earth is bare, One more seed is plant - ed there:

ALTO

Give up your strength the seed to nou - rish, That in course the flow'r may flou - rish

(hum)

(hum or oo)

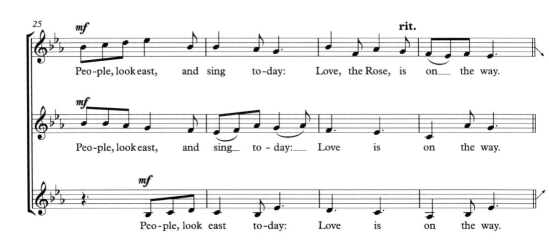

Peo-ple, look east, and sing to-day: Love, the Rose, is on the way.

Peo-ple, look east, and sing to - day: Love is on the way.

Peo-ple, look east to-day: Love is on the way.

4. An-gels an-nounce to man and beast Him who com-eth from the East. Set ev-'ry peak and val-ley hum-ming With the word. The Lord is com-ing!

DESCANT
Sing to-day Love is on the way.

Peo-ple, look east, and sing to-day: Love, the Lord, is on the way.

Two Polish carols

1. Hurrying to Bethlehem

Przybieżeli do Betlejem

trad. Polish
translated Charles Bodman Rae

trad., arr. Witold Lutosławski

praise His__ name.   1. 2. 3. Wel - come lit - tle Je - sus,
na li - rze.   *Wi - ta - ją dzie - cią - tko,*
Him with__ joy.
klę - ka - ją.
set them__ free.
od złe - go.

sent to save and free us, Shep - herds all,
ma - łe pa - cho - ląt - ko, pas - te - rze,

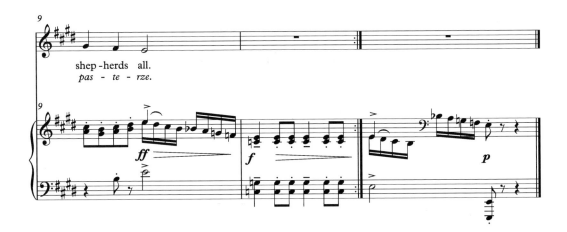

shep -herds all.
pas - te - rze.

2. In a manger
W żłobie leży

trad. Polish
translated Charles Bodman Rae

trad., arr. Witold Lutosławski

VOICES

PIANO

1. In a man - ger,
1. W żło - bie le - ży,
2. Pre - sents bring - ing,
2. My zaś sa - mi

far from dan - ger, lies the child to whom we sing.
ktoż po - bie - ży ko - lę - do - wać ma - łe - mu,
ca - rols sing - ing, we come quick - ly on our way.
zpios - necz - ka - mi za wa - mi poś - pie - szy - my,

Je - sus, new Lord, Christ our true Lord, are you born to
Je - zu - so - wi Chry - stu - so - wi dziś do nas ze -
Ga - ther round all, By the ox stall, There the ti - ny
a tak te - go ma - leń - kie - go niech wszy - scy zo -

For St. Albans Abbey Girls' Choir

Rejoice and be merry

trad., arr. Andrew Parnell

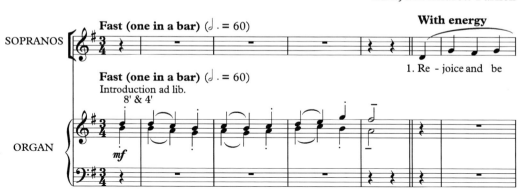

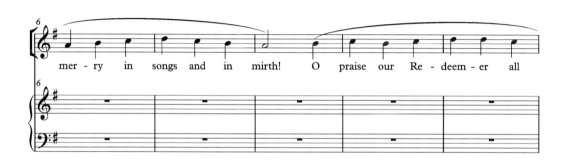

brought us sal - va - tion, his prais - es we'll sing!

8' 2' solo

mf stacc.

mf brightly

3. Like - wise a bright star in the sky did ap -

mf

3. Like - wise a bright star in the sky did ap -

-pear, which led the wise men from the East to draw near; they

-pear, which led the wise men from the East to draw near; they

myrrh, myrrh, in - cense and gold. So bless - ed for

un - to him of - fered myrrh, in - cense and gold. So bless - ed for

e - ver be Je - sus our King,___ Who brought us sal -

e - ver be Je - sus our King, Who brought us sal -

-va - tion, his prais - es we'll sing!___

-va - tion, his prais - es we'll sing!

19-21 xii 1998

The shepherds' farewell
from *The Childhood of Christ*

Berlioz, translated Paul England

Berlioz arr. Basil Ramsey

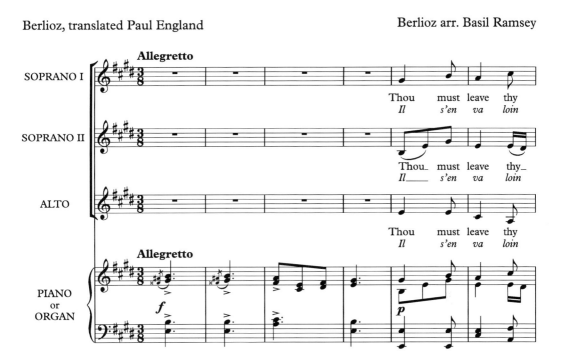

13
poco f
Babe, all mor - tal babes ex - cel - ling, Con - tent our earth - ly
De son père et de sa mè - re Qu'il res - te le con -
Babe, all mor - tal babes ex - cel - ling, Con - tent our earth - ly
De son père et de sa mè - re Qu'il res - te le con -
Babe, all mor - tal babes ex - cel - ling, Con - tent our earth - ly
De son père et de sa mè - re Qu'il res - te le con -
19
p
lot to share, Lov - ing fa - ther, lov - ing mo - ther, Shel - ter
- stant a - mour! Qu'il gran - dis - se, qu'il pros - pè - re Et qu'il
lot to share, Lov - ing fa - ther, lov - ing mo - ther, Shel - ter
- stant a - mour! Qu'il gran - dis - se, qu'il pros - pè - re Et qu'il
lot to share, Lov - ing fa - ther, lov - ing mo - ther, Shel - ter
- stant a - mour! Qu'il gran - dis - se, qu'il pros - pè - re Et qu'il
26
f
mf
thee with ten - der care! Lov - ing fa - ther, lov - ing
soit bon père à son tour. Qu'il gran - dis - se, qu'il pros -
thee with ten - der care! Lov - ing fa - ther, lov - ing
soit bon père à son tour. Qu'il gran - dis - se, qu'il pros -
thee with ten - der care! Lov - ing fa - ther, lov - ing
soit bon père à son tour. Qu'il gran - dis - se, qu'il pros -

Say, where is He born?

from *Christus*

Matthew 2, verses 1-2

Mendelssohn

to a - dore Him, for we have seen,_____ have seen____ His

- dore Him, for we have seen,__ have seen____ His

come to a-dore Him, for we have seen, have seen His

star.

star.

star.

Silent Night

W.G. Rothery: Joseph Mohr

Franz Gruber,
arr. Mark Blatchly

Reproduced by permission of Mark Blatchly

bring - eth light, Sav - ing us___ from sin's___ dark thrall,

Giv - ing life___ and love___ to all, Christ,___ the light of the

world,_____ Christ___ the light of the world.

Still, still, still

trad. German
arr. Barry Rose

Brust dar - brin - gen. Still,__ still,__ still,__ weil's__

Kind - lein__ schla - fen__ will!

FULL SOPRANOS

Schlaf,__ schlaf,__ schlaf,__ mein__ lie - bes__ Kind - lein

ALTO I & II

Schlaf, schlaf, schlaf, mein lie - bes Kind - lein

(The accompaniment can double the Alto part, if needed)

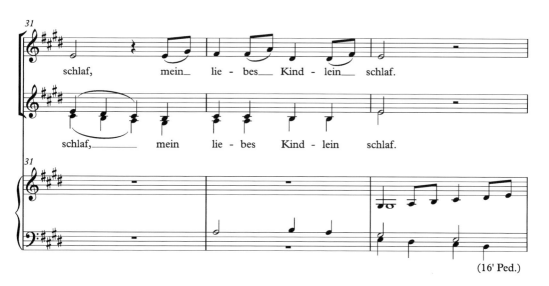

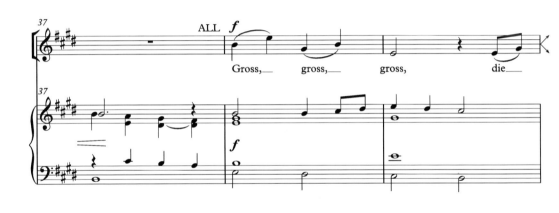

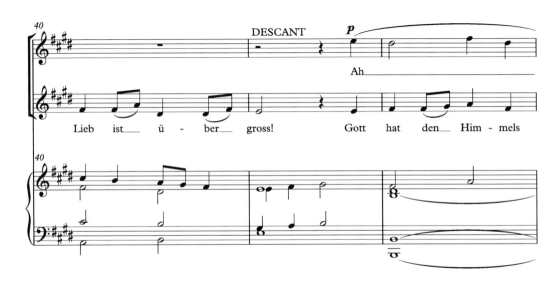

ALL *f*

Gross,— gross,— gross,— die—

DESCANT *p*

Ah——

Lieb ist— ü - ber— gross! Gott hat den— Him - mels

For Dinah and Eve

Sweet was the song

William Ballett

Gerald Hendrie

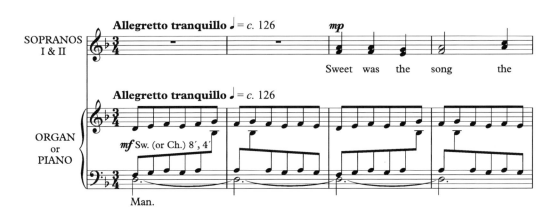

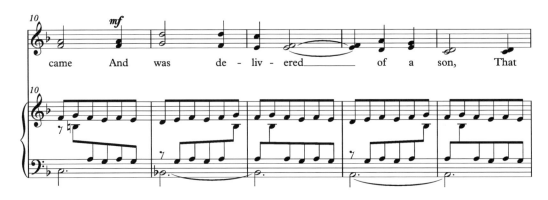

*also

Tomorrow shall be my dancing day

trad., arr. Andrew Carter

O__ my love, This have I done for my__ true love.

love, my love, This have I done for my__ true love._____

In a man - ger laid__ and wrapp'd__ I was, So ve - ry poor,__ this

In a man - ger laid__ and wrapp'd__ I was, So

was__ my chance, Be - twixt an ox and a sil -ly poor ass, To call my true__ love

ve - ry poor,__ This was__ my chance, Be - twixt an ox and a sil -ly poor ass, To

Torches!

trad. Spanish
translated J.B. Trend

John Joubert

For John Abdenour and the choristers of the First United Church of Christ, Milford, USA

Watts's Cradle Hymn

Isaac Watts

Barry Rose

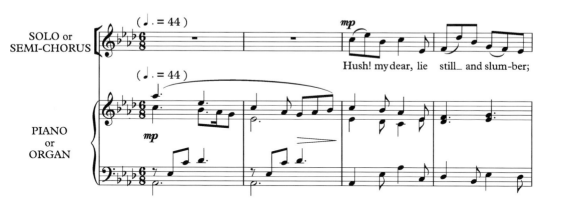

128

Whence is that goodly fragrance flowing?

Quelle est cette odeur agréable?

trad. French
translated A.B. Ramsay

French melody
arr. A.E. Baker

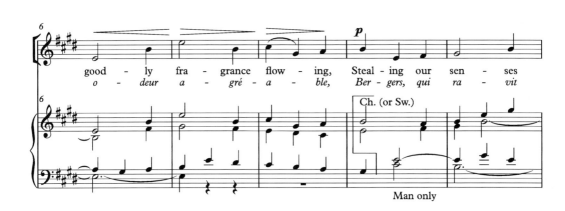

Published by Novello Publishing
Music setting by Stave Origination
Printed in Great Britain